That Other Brightness

That Other Brightness

by
Virginia Gilbert

With a Foreword by Albert Goldbarth

Black Star Press
LINCOLN NEBRASKA

THAT OTHER BRIGHTNESS. Copyright © 1995 by Black Star Press™. All rights reserved. Printed in the United States of America. No part of this book may be used or reproduced in any manner whatsoever without written permission except in the case of brief quotations embodied in critical articles and reviews. For further information contact Black Star Press, PO Box 6165, Lincoln, NE, 68506-0265.

ISBN: 1-887810-40-4

Many of the poems in this book have previously appeared in the following publications: *The Cloverdale Review of Criticism & Poetry 1992, The Daily Iowan, Lincoln Log, Mss., The New York Quarterly, North American Review, Passage, Pebble, Poetry Now, The Poetry Miscellany, The Poetry Society of America Poetry Review, Poets & Peace International Journal, Prairie Schooner, The Red Mountain Review, Southern Poetry Review, Sumac, University of Utah Magazine,* and *Wisconsin Review.*

Some have appeared in the anthologies *New Poets–Women; Anthology 83–A Gathering of Northern Illinois Poets;* and *Cameos: Twelve Small Press Women Poets;* and in the limited editions *To Keep at Bay the Hounds* and *The Earth Above.* "Portraits in Contradiction" has been selected for an anthology of women's poetry forthcoming from Beacon Press.

"For My Father" was the recipient of a 1990 Hackney Literary Award in Poetry, "Birds," won the University of Alabama's 1992 Sakura Festival Haiku Contest, and "Pax Romana" received the Iowa City, Iowa, Coalition's Earth Day Honorarium in 1971.

The author acknowledges the National Endowment of the Arts for its gracious support in the writing of some of these poems.

Cover Photograph: *Li River, China, 1993* by Virginia Gilbert.

For my mother and father
and for those who lead us
towards the light.

December 25, 1995

To Marvin and Marion,

May you have a Merry Christmas and a Happy New Year. I hope you like this book. I love you!

Jenny

LIVING IN LIGHTNING

It was back in the Paleozoic that I first met Ginnie Gilbert—we were ragtag graduate students together in 1969 through 1971. It's twenty-five years later, and I'm pleased to have been asked to introduce her first full-length collection of poems. It hasn't been rushed, that's certain. If anything, it's been carefully nurtured, through rural, weedy Illinois, and various college towns, and urban Korea. I've been a stranger to Ginnie's life through all of those intervening years (and intervening adventures)—our staying-in-touch has been intermittent and brief. But when I read that "We were like people / living in lightning," I remember that Ginnie Gilbert speaks for all of us who live by poetry: we are her constituency.

The range here goes from explorations of family (in "For My Father," the poet evokes "the house of lost goods" and its intimate remains) through immediate musings ("Tonight / on the veranda" one poem begins; and another: "This poem can't make it / out of the kitchen") to a far-flung travel (the poems about Korea, "the women, their dresses / gold-mirrored silk, their sitting, / swan-like, around the stone / borders of ponds. . . " are particularly moving).

And the voice can leap from that of clear anecdotal narrative (". . . Sam / / Smith, farmer, / walked / his fields / for the umpteenth time . . . ") to that of a power-charged dream vision ("Walking in the desert / I entered a low cloud, / I entered the side of a cliff / My body opened / into fossil . . . "), even to that of a shamanistic authority ("It will be like this," one poem begins, a simple poem of prediction with the persuasion of an ancient Sumerian text). There's sometimes a sly, individuated humor here ("Someone needing money / carried my bags, questioning 'Have / you read Whitehead?' 'No, / I have read my hands' . . . ") as well as a willingness to face our human dilemma with unblinking eyes ("The winds carry misfortune," one poem starts out—hard to argue with *that* succinct history lesson).

But what links all this diversity for me is Ginnie's earned, difficult stance as outsider (". . . in a ballroom of people, / / we were people who were / not people"), and the quiet but delightful quirks of language and of strategic decision that this sometimes makes for. Ginnie's work is not radically experimental in the manner of "language poetry"; words are not splattered Jackson Pollock-like over the page, or given an Ashberyesque disjunctiveness. But repeatedly, in ways that remind me of those other outsiders Emily Dickinson and Lorine Niedecker, an integrity of highly personalized expression is preserved.

At its best, this happens in the service of a complex understanding (see, for example, the way the final nine lines of "Hangchou" so ably combine a thrill of fragile beauty with the feel of brute ruthlessness) and in the service of a conscienceful witnessing (see the poignant "Bill Stewart, 1979," or "Memories of Hiroshima").

"The story forgotten is the one / now remembered," Ginnie Gilbert tells us, calling up out of the past, attentive to a poet's work. It's been a rich twenty-five years, in that sense. I'm happy to have been reinvited back into Ginnie's world. You come, too; my guess is you're also "living in lightning."

—Albert Goldbarth

CONTENTS

Living in Lightning   ix
    by Albert Goldbarth

Gate Of Departures

Doing the Nolichucky	5
Barkentine	7
Driving	9
From Konrad Korzeniowski's Diary	14
For John Berryman	15
Wrath	17
Hunters of the Lost Spirit	18
The Keeper of Hours	20

Old Air

For My Father	25
The Last Days	27
The Ritual	29
On the Trip to Russell's Cave	31
Old Air	32
Photographing Bodie	33
The Frontier	35

xiii

Portraits in Contradiction	37
The Drought	39
In the Desert	42
Shaker Town	44

Caught In A Bad Time

The Mozart Poem	49
The Retelling	50
Conversations	51
The Other Side of Myself	53
In That Slow Turn and Lift	55
Returning	56
Momento Mori	58
Caught in a Bad Time	61
The $20 Poem: Hearing the Blues	64

Zero Zone

Birds	71
Impressions at Dawn	72
Outside the Kampongs, at the Market, Waiting	73
In Korea, New Year's Eve, 1971	74
Hangchou	75

At the Monastery of Shining Crystal	76
Memories of Hiroshima	77
Man Rise Night	79
Merchants	80
The Field	82
Upon the Social Unrest in a Foreign Country	83
The Dreaming	84
Bill Stewart, 1979	86
The Pax Romana	87

Not By Earthly Matters Held

A Play in 3 Acts	91
Vanessa	95
The Elegance of First Principles	98
Aurora Australis	100
A Mind of Winter	101
On This, My Birthday, I Think about Emily Dickinson	102
The Sighting	104
The Poetry Writers and Angel Sighting Group's Annual Conference	107
That Other Brightness	109

If I could but describe all that's above:
A rock?
Or the mist coming in?

Gate of Departures

DOING THE NOLICHUCKY

I

Crickets by us
and the water singing
the sky well,
our tents pitched
near the wilderness.
Today I almost stepped
upon a brown toad,
I, at first, not seeing
it, then watched it
jump away—that close
to life and losing it.

II

We throw our rafts
into water, the river
high, everything orange,
our vests, the helmets,
as in an emergency,
as if in danger.
We paddle over rocks,
slide through shoals,
avoid hydraulics, whirlpools.
This is "shooting the rapids,"
the spirit teeth that move
bones to break
and bodies to float.

III

He was found down river,
drowned, when I was four,
from the bridge we crossed
on the way home from school,
a good bridge, too,
of steel and concrete.
There I often stood looking
down at the roaring waters
and I a part of it,
whatever it was, as he,
the curious boy, had become.

IV

We take these risks
to see ourselves
as imagined survived,
as more than the cracked-up
canoe, its bow a splint
of water jammed
upon the rocks. We smell
the carcass of a dead deer
from the far shore. Its
ripe belly has burst forth
butterflies. Their yellow
paths are everywhere,
a necklace of light
surrounding each of us.

BARKENTINE

The winds carry misfortune,
the suffering of tides
where our boat is docked,
so bruised into whiteness
against the pier of our
imaginings. We are harbored
in an alcove of faith
long past the rumors
of conspiracies
where we carry the dark
horizons holding us hostage
like a bracelet so tight
upon the wrist refusing release,
long past the squall we mark,
these gray wails of rain
swelling the sea-grained walls,
the gray-scored earth,
an undulating ribbon
unraveling the water, the two
churning together, the two
a murky conflux
of matter and time,
of motion and force,
of all that dilutes us.
What claim can we
make for the crippled wheel
that once steered us
astray? And what

ships have we lost
to the troubled depths, there
on the floor of our existence,
bottomed out, rusting hulks
of brine? And what identity
is crossed off now
to the lost letter
of entropy? And
what debris will be raised
from our sunken decks,
the splintered plates we ate on,
the knife and fork foraged
from the mud? We cannot count
the mishaps, so many,
and so many, yet we seek
the land, the Norwegian fjord
of steep bays, closed in,
protected, our engines not panicked.

DRIVING

I

So many dead animals on the road,
this four car accident being washed
down in the deepest night, the red
ambulances agog in malky exhalation.
Everywhere I look, someone calls
me to give up this life to noise,
the crash upon silence reverberating
over the fields, the breath path
pushing us on into "wreck."
Which of us turned that fated
corner, now is of no matter,
our countryside mangled into parts.

II

Because it was quiet here,
because I had been gone

the week before, because
in a ballroom of people,

we were people who were
not people, converging

in a name upon our names,
because we stalked the corridors

and ate the dry biscuits,
because we had to eat something,

because we had to wash
down what stuck in our

throats, and when we took
the elevator to those rooms,

to those doors of green
lights, I could not get

my card in, I could not
get past red, because of

the beach and mardi gras,
the celebrations I missed,

the raw clouds and the gulf
between us, that beating

upon the shore, because
I was alone there,

because I am alone here,
my home not home,

because I called you,
because I heard the numbers

click upon my fingers as if
their shorts pulses were

life, and I thought I knew you,
the wordsmith, the singer

as the numbers sing to us
the minute before the sound,

the minute we are waiting
for, the minute to break

the silence of what was before,
the silence that was so loud

inside our heads, inside mine
that day, and so you spoke

of death, of nada,
of your "gigs" with your sons,

of the music, of the rock
and roll of your mouth,

of annihilation, of what
does it matter these small

words of ours made smaller
over the phone, these words

you so loudly said,
these words, I hear these words.

III

It is the motion that moves us, that
quick spin in the new car, that rush
into the next realm that is not
what we are, that is not what goes
with us, that is what keeps us moving,
that is what causes the paradox, the looking
forward, glass upon glass, the eyesight going,
the signs so hard to come by, so hard
to read, the forward movement not really
forward at all, but pressed into ourselves,
pressed into that rear view mirror,
pression and compression of all
that we knew until everything's
a blur small on the horizon,
until everything's everything.

IV

So what do we want tonight,
in this small restaurant, on
this small planet somewhere
on a small patch of the south,
the wreck somewhere out
beyond the tracks, the road
blocked off somewhere inside

ourselves, and the waitress
chatting to us about the collision,
about the people diverting
the traffic away, about
them folks not eating tonight,
about the food we came for,
about that which is ethnic,
about that which is authentic,
and we call for plate
upon plate, for Tom Yum Kai,
for Yum Nue, and Pad Bai Ga-praw,
for that which is spiciest,
so hot upon the palate,
each of us holding in the "ow."

FROM KONRAD KORZENIOWSKI'S DIARY

He was one of us.
—*Joseph Conrad*

It began in the usual way,
with a line close to Europe,
a rugged voyage crossing
the Bering Straits. The sailors
had been long gone
from home; the water
of oceans was carried
in their pockets. In their faces,
I saw the hollow etchings
of straw mats, slept on
and slept on by slender
bodies, the weight
of wind caught in their cheeks.
I have worn their complexion
here, around my leg, a narrow
rope, for years, the binding of my feet
to the dusky swallows
of the coast, the home
I never go back to.

FOR JOHN BERRYMAN

*We must travel in the
direction of our fear.*
—John Morris

The time came
for leaving, the shoes hardened
and the watch given
to Henry down the hall.
Once again, on the journey
to Seoul or Pittsburgh,
the Arena of Rome, the emptied seats,
arched and circular
become a part of our memory.
Wise or small,
the man of the lone eyeglass
honors the ticket
taker with his palm.
This, my friend, at the gate
of departures, is the moment
of our arrival, the people
who have bought the streets,
their undershirts
worn thin, meeting you again
and you, meeting
again and again and again
the conductors of a different
language with one half
of the mustache

left on. Call it fate
or a quick tongue,
the last meanderings
of a forgotten race.
This time, forbear the taxi
or catch it on foot;
a child running by,
fallen into life,
lets his blood flow
into his hands from the pivot
of a broken skull.
This is what you asked
from the gentlest mountain
where, under the squares
of pavements, all our feet
rush pass.

WRATH

In a drunken rage,
the husband microwaves
his wife's kitten.
Like Eliot's bones
buried in the back yard,
a farmer or businessman,
minister or cop,
shoots his son or daughter,
his lover or girlfriend,
hires a mercenary
to bludgeon his woman
across the head,
to throw her into
the shallow grave
or to run her
within her own car
to the bottom of
the nearby lake.
The faceless victims,
the faceless assassins.

In the Pine Barrens,
the boys come upon
her body by accident.
The brown leaves crack
under their feet, not
at all the prey
they were hunting.

HUNTERS OF THE LOST SPIRIT

We came home
to a butcher knife
stuck ominously
into the kitchen
table. Around
the smashed
furniture, decapitated
religious figures
levitated. On March 19,
the apparition
first appeared dressed
as a boy, a white
image. We brought
the priest in, holy
water, high church
incense, a relic
of a saint, and
blessed this house.
Afterward, the rooms
turned icy cold. Luminescent
lights floated on the stairs.
Two hot claws raced
down my wife's cheeks.
Our walls growled.

In truth, we were chased
from our house, from
this phantom laying claim

to us, hunched like
a spectre over our souls
which we would not give.

Oh, those of you
who are innocent, may
laugh at our destiny,
this story, our homelessness,
but this ghost entered
our lives as it may enter
yours, in disguise,
in faces invisible to us,
coming out of discord
to push us one
last immeasurable time
over the railing which we must,
somehow, hang on to
in spite of ourselves.

THE KEEPER OF HOURS

Every day we are destroying ourselves.

—*a Venetian citizen*

Venice is sinking,
the Basilica of San Marco
mirrored in troubled waters.
Wooden planks are walkways;
buildings are lined
in green froth. Under
a canopy of rain, we balance
ourselves along the paths
near the Bridge of the Tree,
over the Street of Assassins
on our way to the Clock Tower,
its soundings, our alarm
to caution. What food
we eat here is long
in coming, passing through
so much water, the cappuccino
and pasta, the broiled fish.
Even hardened into glass,
dolphins swimming on a
store front ledge can break,
perhaps like this city
or the rains against our backs.
Our boats plow up the waves
of our destruction, beating

against the land. Time is
so marked here, like
the pale glow of light
coming from these opaque
windows. We want to look
down those dark corridors
at the layered paintings,
at the silver goblets
on the inlaid chests.
The family crest, embossed
on the wall, is a presence
like a ghost of a child,
rising above it all.

Old Air

FOR MY FATHER

I

Where in the house of lost goods
have gone the yellow scarf and
gold scarab missing since the move?
And in what harbors are the pieces
of shattered glass resting?
Are they beneath the tumultuous storms
that bound the borders of pavements
and cafés? I walked those stones
years ago, up the steps, arches, urns,
and pillars, the walls dark
and darkening with frescoes. So
easily this life falls from us.

II

On the way to Stabiae and to the
inferno's ever deepening silence,
we succumbed to the poisonous gases.
The city was no more than a heap
of rubble, but the citizens rebuilt
in time to meet the volcano's second
roar of lapilli and scoriae. Then
came the lightning, our earthquakes,
the unstable waves of the apocalypse.

III

We rode in chariots shooting arrows
and we pierced the horses' necks
with shouts of "forward, ever forward"
over the barriers and small streams,
the dust road crossing the narrows
of fields and everywhere we felt
the winds, the glorious lost winds.

IV

The story forgotten is the one
now remembered, the passage
of time is the moment now captured.
Beneath a high wall, we dance
in a ring of sun and vision.
These are the months of Red Berries
and Frost on the Grass, the Moon
of the Snowblind and Popping Trees.
What has gone, comes back again
like a long trail through the horizon
before sunrise. Sing to us, oh
brilliant stars, of our existence.

THE LAST DAYS

*With this sad and pitiless fate
we were afflicted.*

—*An anonymous Aztec poet*

Of those events, only these
I remember, that He took
your hand and sent you
to view our city from
the far height of our
Great Temple and from there
you could see with large
advantage the square with crowds
therein buying and selling,
altars and shrines, our flat
roofed houses, and multitudes
of canoes crossing in the canals
off the five causeways leading
into Mexico. A God,
you returned to us
and together we smiled
in each other's company.
Then you lanced through
to death our dancers
seeking rain and strangled
Moctezuma. You fled
into the jungle on the
night of your great defeat
and there you almost starved

and your men sought refuge.
But you gathered our enemies
against us, and returned
to take torch to our houses
and to scatter our grain
and our blood splattered
on the pavement, our animals
fleeing. The rest of us
you sold into slavery,
the price of a poor man
two handfuls of corn, and you
brought us bowed down
unto your God of gold
and lost harmony and there
we gave over to you whatever
we still knew for souls.

THE RITUAL

        We can't be sure what
        their meaning was, but we
        can be sure they had meaning.

At the beginning, before I was nothing,
the great sky swelled my happiness.

        Most figures are composed
        of a single line that never
        crosses itself, perhaps
        the path of a ritual maze.

For this reason, I left my hut
outside the barrios in the pre-dawn
of my existence, the new moon white
upon its shoulders.

        If so, when the Nazcas walked
        the line, they could have felt
        they were absorbing the essence
        of whatever the drawing symbolized.

In this distant ghostly light
I went to the fields to note
my life, the marks upon the sands.

        For according to their ways
        of thinking, a man's life-force,
        or soul, resided in his head.

*So, cracking two skulls together,
I prayed for fertility, the freedom
from boredom. My anthropomorphic hands
held no fat, it being the dry season.*

                        I shall bring you people
                        without knees and they will
                        defeat you.

*They will defeat you, these gods
of the earth. The rain judges
our renewal.*

ON THE TRIP TO RUSSELL'S CAVE

If this is where I start out,
on the edge of the cracked skull,
the cerebellum sliced off,
the loculus of motion left
circularizing behind, then
what beast creeps ahead?
This morning, the fine rain
beads on the head
of my brown car. My two dogs
peer after me. Here, vegetation
lies all around. I lift one
muddy boot after the other
out of the mire, pushing forward
to the cave, the burial mound,
the archaeological dig. Goats
have claimed the overhanging cliff.
The old ranger cracks a walnut
with flint; its skin is
the feel of brain, the crevices
are etched with the knuckles of brain,
this reasoning of grooves
which he now gives so causally to me.

OLD AIR

Randy Cofer, drilling in coffins,
tries to withdraw a trace of air;
have man-made chemicals altered
the atmosphere? The leaden box
sits plumply on its casings
and does not answer. So much
weight from the past protecting
the unpolluted rotting man
inside! Yet, the air is rarefied;
no industry there, just the
bone knitting of the dead.

Others have tried for pristine
samples before, old wine bottles,
glacial ice, air bubbles in glass,
but to no avail: it's hard
catching such air—so illusive,
so invisible. The fiberoptic
camera pokes its eye around
the well-preserved skull
with skin and thin black hair;
its long tentacle reaches
down to the well-buttoned coat,
the bully vest, slides
beside the breeches, scales
the foot with shoe and buckle.
What we see is what we see;
it's all a velvet lining of dust,
and no room for breathing.

PHOTOGRAPHING BODIE

Everything was left in place
in that high town dug so deeply
underground, the magazines
on the rack, billiard cues
on the table, the drinks
still set, a world map
schooling you to new mines.
But what gain was there
in Bodie? The corrugated
buildings housed the fortune
grinding everything down
for that moment of gold.
Now the brilliant light,
thinned by snow and dry wind,
heat and cold, polarizes
the gaming wheel, your last
poker chips. Coffins and
sewing machines, typewriters,
skis, a violin, its pieces
all unglued by dust, do
the speaking for you
as if you cast them down
like demons unto the earth,
a scar in the Nevadas cut
in haste, sick with altitude,
dehydrated, your bones chilled.
The human eye tries to correct
the colors here, find the contrast,

make up the difference with
filters, but we know the truth,
of the fires consuming you,
street by street, shop by horrid
shop, so violent a struggle
between you and the outside.
We mourn you isolated
in your death, arrested
in your frenzy to get somewhere,
torn by need. Did you find
what you were after? Or is it still
buried beneath you like
some mother lode never found?

THE FRONTIER

Buffalo hides and beaver pelts
stank where flies swarmed
inside the fort. Yet, in
the distance, its hunched
shadow was like a raised
shield to us, we having crossed
the great desert by wagon
and foot for three weeks
straight under threat of attack
and hardship, our spirits
flattened. When the others
left, I chose to stay
with an officer offering
me shelter. There was order
here, a picket fence
and stone houses, washer
women down at the stream.
The captain married us
against the sun-glared horizon,
and we lived our days
like white lightning. Then
at Twin Forks, there
was an encounter, my man
among the dead; my soul
became a great cave, and my
spirit riding, riding the gray
mare into the hills. You
who spot me now say I am

a vision, the wind that circles
like a howl, the dust filling
my skirt. I long so to hold
the objects of the earth.
Where can I touch them?

PORTRAITS IN CONTRADICTION

Since I cannot speak of fields
and broken fences where the
winds howl, I speak instead of
how we did not speak and went
our separate ways across the
plains; the cow grass whipped under
the rims of our cast iron wheels,
you up the hill, and I straight
ahead towards the Big Bottom,
four clear lines in opposite
direction. You chose the sun
in a western window, I
the spectre moon, you built of
bricks, I of reeds and cattails,
and we endured thirty years
each in our own ways of not
talking. You hired men, bought
cattle, started a ranch. I
cleared the land, kept a bird, rocked
on the porch. You worked numbers,
expanded, I grew into
myself. You made money, joined
the club, became mayor, I
worked the loom, sending shuttle
over warp and woof, stick and
fiber. While you threw parties

and danced in a circle, I
threw my carpet on the dirt
floor and walked the tree of life.

THE DROUGHT

It was
the morning
before
it rained,
and Sam Smith,

farmer,
expected nothing
from the clumps
of clay.
And Sam

Smith, farmer,
walked
his fields
for the umpteenth
time, for

the seven
years' worth
of dryness
he felt
flaking

from his skin
like pieces
of bark
flaking
from the dead

cottonwood,
his mother's
tree. And Sam
Smith, farmer,
knew

the precise
smell
of cattle
rotting, locust
like, by

the stock tanks,
near the caved–
in wells,
the long
forgotten streams.

And where
the earth
smelled
of heat, Sam
Smith knew

the suffering
of a sun
set
too high,
knew

the dust-
filled streets.
And Sam Smith,
a farmer,
searched

for a sign –
a stubborn
hawk rising
out
of the sullen

sky.

IN THE DESERT

I

Walking in the desert,
I entered a low cloud,
I entered the side of a cliff.
My body opened
into fossils. My body
hardened into crystal.
The weather longed
for change. When a gully
split along my spine,
the animals, dying of heat,
entered me. I long to be
the cave of winter. Somewhere,
on the shelf
of the Mediterranean,
treasures drift,
compacted in seaweed,
the slow dance back, back
and forth.

II

This is the second part. Around
the Mulberry bush, I asked
many questions but I did not
know the language. People
handed me papers. Someone
sat me down beneath

the river. He said, "Look,
you need trouble,
you need rocks,
inlaid pottery,
a German complexion." I felt
the water come over me, then.
I was the dam, a beaver's nest,
the perpetual fall
into mountains,
always disappearing.

III

When my mother died,
I was in the army.
I was writing poetry.
We lived in a tent. We had
no water. We had no indoor
plumbing. I slept on a
wooden bench. Tell me,
what is the marrow
of your complexion so that
I can write it down.
I wear my clothing
in the evening,
when I am waking.

SHAKER TOWN

I

Dost ever thou think
O darling fair loved one
of the last time we stood linked
in each other's embrace
but think as thou goest on thy way
of that time when my heart
was so full of love overflowing
that I spoke not but kissed thee
and sent thee away?

> —*Shaker Poem, Wall of Room 174*
> *Old Stone Shop*
> *West Family*
> *Pleasant Hill, Kentucky*
> *anon.*

II

Perhaps a pale fall night,
leaves in a flurry against
the door, its wood creaking
with the battering, an opening
to the poem inside: Job's
troubles troubling you, eating
in silence, having to look
away. "We are thankfull
for the blessings so bountifully

bestowed. . . ." In the cutting
and stacking of hay, in
the preserving of fruits,
we store up our labors,
but your preparation was
for something else.
I'm sure you called it
"releasement," falling
into song, such Simple Gifts
gathering into yourself
like ripe plums bursting
open. What love whirls
on Holy Sinai's Plains?
All I see are ghosts –
the words on the wall
and chairs meant
for angels to sit in.

Caught in a Bad Time

THE MOZART POEM

Joseph II: There are simply too many notes.

Mozart: There are just as many notes, Majesty, neither more nor less, as are required.

—from Amadeus *by Peter Shaffer*

Though you ask me to give up
this blue hatching, I cannot and watch
it fold the language in upon itself
somewhat like the waters turning
round the stars in air or mitre
joint in the ground. And if this choosing
opens the gates to sound, so let
it be the broken fence of mail
upon the wind that fails to keep
at bay the hounds. I take such pleasure
from a field where only vastness can be found.

THE RETELLING

All I know is that
my poetry is more
than cowboys fighting
in a saloon or stepping
in cow dung. No mother
enters my kitchen to clean
up the dishes or to teach
me how to sew. In my family,
we don't break bread
together or go to town
in the pickup to catch
a Saturday matinee.
Grain elevators explode
on someone else's
horizons, not mine
and when I see the sun
rise, it is because
a friend calls from overseas,
not because I have to farm.
I was the one who never
played house and gave
the doll away and when
my dad broke my toy guitar,
I tried, like all the king's
horses, to put it together
again. All I know is that
in my pen there is light
and darkness and that
we go through both.

CONVERSATIONS

Midnight and my phones
chirp again like kids (birds)
for a few brief moments
as if the line is somewhere
in agony. What is this
wire, anyhow, that connects
my heart with yours
or to another? The white
cord is harmless enough
in itself, almost coldly
antiseptic, running, really,
to nothing but a hole.
Yet, it speaks in the garbled
sounds of a thousand
parameters all converging
on each other, a Babel
of poems collapsing into words.
We are all the same
on the phone, each of us
bodiless voices. Some
of us are wrong numbers.
We look into the mask
of anonymity lost
in a crowd and call
it insult. Others call it
work. It makes us question
love in its silence;
anxious, it is the dark

chortle of help. Such rude awakening is out of blankness into self. Listen—we can almost hear the breathing.

THE OTHER SIDE OF MYSELF

is always missing
at appointments.
I conduct the
interviews finding
no one to answer
my questions, no one
to hire or fire,
and she, in turn,
finds it easy
not to answer,
having nothing
to say, but rather,
enjoys the blank
wall's image of
herself. I lean
back into my chair,
sighing, then wave
my hand through the
empty air, pointing
out the company's
decline, the loss
of production. I
exclaim that parts
are incomplete,
can't be shipped,
mention workers
are idle. She
doesn't care, pays

little attention,
is distracted.
I get frustrated,
yell for help, but
she is already
gone on vacation,
the door open
and the muzak
getting louder.

IN THAT SLOW TURN & LIFT

This poem can't make it
out of the kitchen. It crawls
in the pots and pans, bangs them
together, tries to climb out.
Neatly stacked plates show
the way, know the exits,
tell the words where
to lie down and be eaten.

RETURNING

I

Tonight
on the veranda
I think about happiness,
how it enters the houses
in darkness
lost in sleep. Night hawks
wander the street lights;
crickets punctuate
the walking of the cat.
I note myself:
the veins in my wrists
and how they protrude
as the skin closes in,
how the porch swing
creaks now. The summer
yawning has overtaken
me and I rejoice
in the small comforts
of root juices,
of light leaving the window,
of the mosquito's bite
awakening me to pain.

II

I used to think
it was my drunken

father to blame:
how I fought him,
ten and angry,
on top of him.
He said
it was not right
to hit him,
a working man,
in the face
and so I never
aimed for that
but something else,
beyond him.

III

Tonight
on the veranda
I think about happiness,
about people
in their houses.
I am not them:
I am the evening,
white paint
peeling from the ceiling.

MEMENTO MORI

*The idea of the circle does not
change in its essence.*
— St. Augustine

*I fight myself stepping on
the throat of my own voice.*
—Yevgeny Yevtushenko

I

Where have I been all these
days? Tonight the violet
skies strain with discord, speaking
of the first winter storm,
the wind carrying off
the last remaining leaves,
leaving everything bare.
Where the heavens cling through
the hollows of clouds, I
see Aquarius falling
from its square of darkness
upon the spaces below.
I don't know how long now
it has been since I have
wanted to say anything.
So many seasons come
and go without feeling
except for dedication

to work. I welcome this
change, oh Gods, violent and
gray, that forces commitment
to something else.

II

In the museum of bone, the
bones are stationary, brown
and propped, held up by wires.
Here, the head of the tallest
mastodon in the world is
elongated, flat, its tusks
almost crossing in mid-air.
Above the door hangs a giant
oceanic turtle now extinct;
its feet reach out like human hands.

III

Peach, I came across a picture
of you given to me last summer.
You were panning for gold
in Colorado. Bent over,
your feet are propped
against the rocks. The
eternal weakness at
the heart is the fear
of falling in. The problem
with evil is that we
have to speak cautiously,

not saying too much
or too little. On the River
of Doubt, the trees
are always bending
towards the foul weather
inside all of us.

IV

There, in autumn's riot,
is assassination and firebombing;
all our words are torn down
and the vital lines broken,
the poetry burnt in the presses.
In this land of no rewards,
we stay hidden in a place
almost resembling a room,
the beginning like the end.
Oh Shadow, the majestic stare,
the foul crossbone of zero!
Remember the difficulty
and come unto your art.

CAUGHT IN A BAD TIME

I

We are punished
for the sins of our fathers.
An alcoholic's daughter
becomes alcoholic, a drunk's
children learn to expect
the hidden bottles, the middle
night arguments, the irrational
chaos slams down upon us.

II

When it was time for bed
(for her life had come
to that), she wondered if there
were not different sets of eyes
for understanding. The fanatics
told her to pray for salvation
and she wanted so hard
to believe that all she had
to do was give in, if she
only could, to give in
if she only could.

III

Lying in green light,
she looked at what

she held in her hands,
the mummy wrapped
in brittle shroud,
the soul gone but the body
remains, now a thousand years
of weight pressed against
the box, the sun transfixed
in the plaster above its head;
no, not death but sadness
was cast in the eyes looking down.

On the frozen river, the toothless
hag takes the casket that holds
her beauty and smashes it
against the ice.

IV

In the deep underground
where all our follies and sorrows
are stored, we cannot tell
if it is morning or night.
Words turn to dust and
are swept away. In
that slow twist and turn,
we grasp for a rock, a wall,
something to hold on to.

V

Out where the dogs are barking
beyond the 3 a. m. darkness,

Bald Mountain lies in mist,
the moon mad-cap in the purple
sky. On this, the first autumn cold,
we search for Orion's clear, burning light.

THE $20 POEM: HEARING THE BLUES

My dad hung out
in bars and all
through school I
dragged him from
them, sent in
by my mother
to get him home.
A bartender he
once was
at the Picnic
Grove on the Fox
River, mixing drinks
in his starched
white shirt
and vest
as if nothing
was wrong,
a cocktail shaker
between his hands
and the bottles
behind him sparking
in the light,
his customers
leaning on
the mahogany bar.

This is
an inheritance,

90 year old
Grandpa Gilbert,
no longer knowing
the grandkids'
names, still
recited every
barroom verse
from memory,
not a word lost.
Grandpa sang
with his brother
Webster, the
vaudevillian
who died
from drink.

I don't go
to bars much
now, but tonight
I want to hear
someone almost
famous sing at a
place so small
and crowded
I have to sit
at the bar.
I feel like
my dad on
this stool,
joking with

the bartender,
comparing him
with the picture
I have, looking
at the bottles
all lined up,
the postcards,
potato chips
and popcorn
bags hanging
from the
paneled walls.

The bartender
is concerned,
seeing me write
on the napkin,
not looking
at the singer,
and he lightly
touches my arm
with his fingers,
asking me if
I am alright.

I'm doing fine,
dad. If I could
but drag you here
now and not be
so grave, we

could claim
back what was
ours. This glass
is for you, dad.
The poem belongs
to all of us.

Zero Zone

BIRDS

In a far field cranes
under a drape of rain bend
white wings, folding moons.

IMPRESSIONS AT DAWN

Here is the wooden
dirt bridge. And here
is the old man, laconic,
his ox and his cart
crossing. There is the sky,
a small branch
in his vest pocket.

OUTSIDE THE KAMPONGS, AT THE MARKET, WAITING

to Mrs. B.

The shopkeeper hands you
a key. It is to a box

of black lacquer, a storm
painted on it, a crane

long-necking down the mote
to the darkness where

the reeds are hollowing
into a distant sea.

IN KOREA, NEW YEAR'S EVE, 1971

The weather forecast
for the Republic is partially sunny.
Today, I am the tourist
come to see the greatness
of the Boulevard, the Southern Gate.
In the garden where parties
were held and by the Pagoda
in front of the Palace steps,
I kneel beside the Dragons
broken into rocks. Think
of the women, their dresses
gold-mirrored silk, their sitting,
swan-like, around the stone
borders of ponds, the King,
maybe drinking too much
and faint, playing with the hand
of someone nearby, the Prince
whose youth kept him out
beside a tree in his ceremonial garb.
Today I am the tourist
out of season. I have the garden
to myself, secret, its old trees
twisted and empty, the people cold
and at home. This midnight
I will toss off my head
with drinking, round and loving
the ancestors whose bones
clang with me, dark, small,
white in the center of my life.

HANGCHOU

We walked so much
in the rain this summer,
along the lake and the rock
gardens, the frogs bloating
to the surface, and the cicadas
harnessed in their boxes,
calling us as if in one
loud voice to seek shelter
in that awful hotel strong
with mildew and cockroach,
stained carpet and baby bird—
roasted beak and all. Its
little mouth perched so open
at us, and for some it was
a great delicacy and for others
something that could not be
looked at. How do we eat
a thing so young, so small,
so complete in death?
Everywhere in China we saw
scrolls of wild horses galloping
towards us, their manes and tails
flashing excitedly in their run,
sometimes stepping on swallows,
on the verge of crushing them—
such power in beauty, such
beauty in power! Must
it always be like this?

AT THE MONASTERY OF SHINING CRYSTAL

Achintya, "The One Beyond Thought,"
spoke at the moment of birth
under the haze of morning. "Like rain,"
he said, "is the sparrow, falling
and rising, gloriously the bird
of heaven." So he told me
to hold the bell firmly
in my grip, in the zero zone
of compassion and wisdom
where the sacred skull is
a vessel transforming evil
into good. How opposite
is the letter of man
speaking of death, of the
bloody house's lost
dimension where souls
burn in the mystical triangle,
not knowing the center of the earth.

MEMORIES OF HIROSHIMA

*1. When it happened, the shadows
of things were left behind.*

*2. Within two weeks, flowers
began to grow.*

(how it might have been)

And this is that place where I see myself,
in the day's light, by the black pool
of your heart, emerging. And this
is that time, a silent bottle breaking
in our heads, the houses on our backs.

(the minute before)

There was the expected normalcy
of the day; the sun was out
and there were no predictions
of rain. Workers were already
in the shipyard and a group
of our boys had gone
down near the center of town
to dig some ditches.
There was no warning.

(after the wind)

My sandals were burnt
to my feet and fragments
of teeth were sown into my skin.

What I saw
were the shadows of things.

人 出 夜
(MAN RISE NIGHT)

The turning of light
towards heaven is what

night sets in our bones.
Our wives hollow out

the houses of our thoughts
by the mountain streams,

quiet by the moon bird's
flight. Sing to the Cassia's

startled mountain flowers
when the earth springs

in the middle of our bellies.
We are rising to the emptiness

of fall.

MERCHANTS

I

The myth
of the Valley

of the Assassins
is that it is

not far
from our backs.

Away from
the green lands,

agents
of the king

carrying gold
in pockets

of the skin, stop
at streams

for drinks, unbuckling
their swords before

bending down. When
it happens, it

is unexpected.

II

At the market,
buying gold,

women move cloaked
in the pale,

afternoon sun.
Shopkeepers throw

water on
calves hung

in windows. Pigs'
heads and lambs'

are gutted. Blood
from a chicken

is a water–
fall over

the curb's
ledge.

THE FIELD

They were walking out
to the field
where it used to happen
on normal days
so many years ago,
now grown over
with weeds, first along
the dirt road, then somewhere
beneath the rise
of a low hill a ditch,
the left-over ashes, soggy,
clumped in a pile like so
much burnt wood.
"These are human," she said,
"Look. Can you believe it?"

UPON THE SOCIAL UNREST IN A FOREIGN COUNTRY

Because we were in a country
under siege, and the roads
were closing, we could not dream.
Everywhere, the lights were going out;
the wind swept fall dust clouds
into the city and we could not see.

The images of men and women,
the image of people having images
are all dying now in the shadows
of the streets.

Goya pictured it well
in times of trial,
the firing squad of lost hopes,
senseless despair. Words
of change, so long kept shut,
are said in violence.

A time ago when body
and mind were one,
the only guns held over us
were our own souls
and the blue skies shining.

THE DREAMING

for Jean Waddell, Anglican
missionary to Iran, 1981

I

It was the year the world
fell apart. Everyone
said that. Reading in bed
on pillows not right
for my head (a cramp
in my neck), the pictures I saw
swelled with gasoline
fires and broken windows
someplace else: in Italy
this spring, riding
a crowded train, I read quietly
The Sights of Rome when a rock
came slamming through ours.
We froze before we jumped
to the floor. I thought
it was a shot. Silent,
we got up, picking
glass out of our hair.
I had a splinter in my
right eye. "That's
what I get for reading,"
I said. We looked
at the hole, the cracked

mirror behind the middle seat,
at the shattered fragments
sprayed across the compartment.
There on the squat, wooden table,
one orange glass of prim soda
miraculously still sat.

II

In the other country
I left behind, men were entering
Jean's apartment to strangle her,
then three bullet wounds
to the chest. Somewhere
she goes on living in a hospital
or in a dream, yours or mine.

III

I was sleeping in the afternoon
because it was hot and the heat
took the energy out of me.
The bedroom door was open
to catch the breeze
and from it came a whisper
of someone calling me
to, at last, get up.

BILL STEWART, 1979

Imagination fails me now
for the facts are too bright
to be ignored, the newsreel,
the camera, the tropical sun,
a troop of soldiers, a newsman
lying face-down in the dust
of a road, a commando questioning,
then kicking, him. We know the pain.

This world talks of freedom.
In the haze, under the lamplights
the paved walk is empty,
and everything is in black and white.

THE PAX ROMANA

It will be like this.
The sky will be rubber gray,
rocks will be leveled
and birds will go underground.
Sand will crawl
across the face
of the earth and fog
will chew branches off trees.
In the early stages,
pine cones will be sold
in stores and fishing rods
will become a popular
wall decoration. The water
level will rise. Libraries
will dissemble, words will
float, become saturated,
peel off their pages,
and, the pages will be
dumb, a layer of silt
drifting to the bottom.
In the end,
there will be no source.
Water will be everywhere.

Not By Earthly Matters Held

A PLAY IN 3 ACTS

*The burden was not taken from me
but I was taken from the burden.*
—Pastor Christian Reger, #26 661

Act I

Not the flight of birds
nor the journey into the wilderness
but the fall of rain, the gutters flooded.
At long last the tide whirls into
the wind's circle, into the leaves
caught in motion. Boots
are not enough; the old paraphernalia
of storms is remorse, the gray sky over trees
in the forest, close to winter.

Today I am thinking about those
found in history, what happens
when the light is sent out
from a different head seeing
the world as round, the intellect
routed to further ends of forget,
what wiser bodies have endured. Each
has stood in front of us, as shape
revealing shape but nothing more; they could not
compromise the soul's neglect. Those
who have fallen off the earth
are not by earthly matters held.

So it was for Galileo bent
on one knee in front of the city square,
so it is now.

Act II

Through the lightness of my eyes,
I have come to Jerusalem
to live. The Via Dolorosa lies
beneath the balcony. Below
is where Christ first fell. On this,
a sunny day, the valley is flourishing
with flowers.

Whoever is contaminated in spirit,
whoever is too weak to stand straight, he
who is contaminated in his flesh,
scarred in the feet or the hands,
deaf, blind, or dumb, cannot occupy
a seat in the congregation which is a room
we all must enter before leaving.

We talked of bodies, of their weight
upon each other. You are thin.
You do not feel the earth's pull.
I am heavy. It is no coincidence.

Seeing: that is important;
the sky in its place.
Here, in this world, we treasure rocks.
When the new moon comes earlier

than expected, the strangeness
of our faces cannot touch it.

Act III

Although I have come and gone
and come again to the expectation
of sound, there is something
I do not hear that is more
than the lifting of my hand
or head in your direction.
In my mind is a scene.
The bulrushes are parting
along the river where a rowboat
with a young girl heads desperately
for shore. A haze has been forming
on the bridge and the delicate neck
of a crane bends gracefully forward
under a drape of rain.

Dearest Claire, is it true
you are sick and can't be found? This
is a strange country, and although
you speak the language, you don't
know your way around.

The night I arrived in London,
it was hit by a cold front. I looked
for the right direction, tired

of carrying my own suitcases. A man
was pushing an empty cart. Outside Munich,
at Dachau that day, I had listened to one
of us tell his story, tell us
that we have our own stories
to tell. This is mine.
On a strange night, I met
a strange man who had bombed
Munich into the Alps.
The beerhalls filled with snow,
the famous Glockenspiel stopped.
In a near field, we
could not even ask for bread.

Not the first time but the second
awakening, in a dream, looking
to where the universe is moving,
I saw what was missing.
Someone needing money carried
my bags, questioning, "Have
you read Whitehead?" "No,
I have read my hands," I joked,
and, "Why are you doing this?"
I continued. "Nothing better to do,"
he said, "nothing better to do."

I call them chance that has survived.

VANESSA

If once nearing dark, Vanessa,
walking the bridge down,
stopped someone passing by,
she would pull her shawl
tightly around in front of her
and with her one free hand
ask the gentleman
for a cigarette,
there under the early
lights and rising fog,
not knowing what else
to ask for
nor where to walk,
it being more
like habit
than anything else.

The arches,
thirty-three in all,
were built for Christ's
life, and now they were
unfurling before her,
a glimmering white
like an ascension
into heaven except
for the smell of urine
where the old men pissed.
But there were the reeds,

the small eddies,
and mud shoals,
and somewhere behind
it all beyond reach
a sun setting
like a bayonet.

And on the bridge
itself were salesmen
with carpets slung
over their backs, their
multicolored mats thrown
over the railing, and vendors
clipping the loud pieces
of candy with their shears;
down the sides, stalls
of gold dealers were
weighing and balancing
until it was dark,
dark and silent.

Her house was dark
and silent, too,
inside her, carried
with her, but outside
she realized was fire,
in the horizon, the bon-fires,
a crisp snapping
awakening of flame.

Isn't this, oh, Lord,
the flicker we are after?

THE ELEGANCE OF FIRST PRINCIPLES

Polished rock blued by the incessant rains
gleam of jeweled chambers to interior realms.

Where I found you I have long forgotten,
somewhere in that distant past, perhaps

as a child not seeking beauty, but finding
it happen chance on an unforseen morning,

maybe sometime when the sun blazed a clear
dawn daring the somber clouds to run away.

A song sang then through the weathered trees
of such melodies that those of another age

could only identify, but, to me, it came
as a whisper of a new awakening far from

people, an echo almost, of a deeper longing
that, somehow, reverberated, that somehow grew

louder as I listened to it, and there, I entered
that lapis lazuli world of your being, that

world of pure color and form, of symmetry,
of symbolism, of symphony, of sympathy,

of symbiosis. Tonight, I lift you off
the bookshelf, still perfect in your creation,

still hard and enduring, a continuous reminder
of your patience and survival, your edges catching

the low light and sending it inward towards
your hollowed center. Every angle crystalizes,

illuminating this lingering darkness like fire flies,
like fire flies, like fire flies and, in this doing,

it is not you, but I who have been seized,
and, in the besieging, I, too, have been set free.

AURORA AUSTRALIS

They come from stumps, the
Great Southern, mule-eared,

type cast from matrices,
saxatile, mahoganied mound builders.

Cloistered in their death-runes,
these celestial blue babies

are the apocryphal prayer wheels
of continents, pillars of armor

dragonally crossing the Kingfisher
Trader. Barter there these

igneous rocks, those marbleized
chimes, malachite, lapis,

sapphirine, converging, unripe,
with the sea, breaking, somewhere,

a barrier, off the reef. So
call us now to that lamenting,

this song of basket weavers
threading their green pearls,

circuitously, across
the juniper skies.

A MIND OF WINTER

A sprinkling of snow ever so slight
fell on a green jade bowl, translucent,
placed on the ground the night before
under a half moon light by God knows whom.

In the mountains a delicate bowl like this
would be buried in snow, its beauty lost
under the vast whiteness, but here,
in front of the house, joined in a dance
of bird tracks, it is a small glistening sight.

By noon, such wonders will be gone, perhaps
an imaginary glance dissolved in sun,
but I knew it once, a silent visitation
of width and breath, a brief life
like a hand held out momentarily, then falls.

ON THIS, MY BIRTHDAY, I THINK ABOUT EMILY DICKINSON

We are both December children
born in the cold behind
the hemlock hedges lost
in the eternity of snow,
and all the gates closed.
Where flits your shadow now
in these shuttered woods?

Two years ago in rain,
I stood on the road
searching for it,
visitor hours too short
and gone, like you –
I cannot enter, shut out
to that inner world housing
your circumference where poems grew
beneath your corner window,
like flowers, salamanders,
each a slender fellow
in the grass, a slant of light.
Red brick still walls you off –
not even Susan could break through.

A wrought iron fence surrounds
your small marker, separate
in the grave, green skies fraught

with thunder, a funeral in the brain—
we must each let go. Is there peace
there, dressed in the white of no
abstractions? Now caught in marriage,
you have the privilege to die.
May the Lord not shut you in the cold.

THE SIGHTING

for Elaine, who keeps watch

It had been a day lost to me,
I, coming home late, full of drink,
hearing the trees roar, God's
heavy hand against me. Then
in my sweat, I threw off my clothes
and dove in our black pool
near midnight, free floating,
drifting to the edge and back again.
I looked up into the night,
the full moon above the shed,
stars and pale clouds
overhead, when I saw
a hazy ball of light drop
in a fall of uncertain distance
straight down before it leveled
off and shot to the left,
an act I knew not reasonable,
sending me scrambling
to the house for glasses
and binoculars. I
scanned the skies for another
sighting, maybe an hour,
and I became a voice
speaking to myself, saying
"Here, and here, and here,
no sign is written," and

"It is useless," and my spirit
made defeat. In the widening
circle of wind, I grew restless,
wanting to give up. "Oh, you
of little faith," I said,
as I peered in the direction
the strange object had gone.
Over the city lights and ground
clutter, over the glare from
the lit tennis courts and the
parking lots, I saw in my lens
it suddenly appear again
from an empty sky with a sister
ship, and again disappear, again
appear before they hovered
perfectly still in unison and
I could see them only in the glass,
settled there, over us, unknown
to the others, unbelievable,
and I broke into a run to the house
and phone, trying to rouse friends,
to tell them to rise and see.
By the time I returned, the vision
was gone, and I stayed the night
looking in one corner and then
the next, and I asked, "Are they
barbaric or strange or nightmare
creatures, and what primitive slime
did they come from or go to, and will they
return? Let them return." I have seen
them since but once, in the expanse

of Indiana field and road
and deserted night, they maybe
observing me in their distances
and I them in mine across the great
dark, and I wonder
if we could cut through sight,
would we find the language of salvation
and would we, at that point
of creation, know ourselves?

THE POETRY WRITERS AND ANGEL SIGHTING GROUP'S ANNUAL CONFERENCE

We were like people
living in lightning,
waiting for the great fall
that summer day
out in the broad west
so far from town.
In the slit canyons
of northern Arizona,
we set our sights
upward through the
spiraling center of vision
past the slickrock domes
and spires where light
shimmered down deep
into the crevices, turning
everything into the liquid
lake of our imagination.
We could not write, then,
until the angel came
so glaringly upon us,
its winged arms cascading
over the sculpted sides
of ancient stone. Some
of the men shrieked
and fell to their knees
on the hard rock,
so lost in prayer,

speaking in tongues
in the madness
that followed.
Our voices, like
a matin, were of birds
floating above us,
battering their bruised
bodies against the foreign
walls into awakening;
our hearts blazed into Heaven,
the words rising above us,
so humbled into brightness.

THAT OTHER BRIGHTNESS

This could be my day
when, perhaps walking

under the trees through
all the blooded leaves

fallen on the sidewalk,
I call it quits, maybe

not by choice, but
by accident, like

this ground squirrel
bowled over by the road,

down on its back, its paws
still twitching and all

its red force splattering
out onto the pavement.

Why is there always
that one death to bear,

isolated on the street,
its own beauty marring

that other brightness
caught in its slow motion

downward into the unknown
regions of the heart?

Virginia Gilbert grew up in the Northern Chicago suburb of Cary, Illinois, along the beautiful Fox River. She has a B.A. in English from Iowa Wesleyan College, an M.F.A. in Creative Writing/Poetry from the Iowa Writers' Workshop, and a Ph.D. in Creative Writing/English from the University of Nebraska. Over the years, she has studied the craft of poetry writing with such notable poets as Ellen Bryant Voigt, Marvin Bell, Galway Kinnell, George Starbuck, Kathleen Fraser, David Ray, and Greg Kuzma.

Virginia has taught both in the United States (University of Utah, College Lake County, Illinois, the University of Nebraska, and Alabama A&M University) and overseas, first with the Peace Corps in the Republic of South Korea, and later with several American companies in Iran before she was evacuated from that country after the overthrow of the Shah in 1978.

She has received numerous awards in both writing and photography including a National Endowment for the Arts grant, a Hackney Award, a Kodak Special Merit Award, and a Fulbright scholarship to China. Presently, she is an Associate Professor of English at Alabama A.&M. University in Huntsville where she teaches and directs its developing creative writing program.

The fonts used in this book are Bodoni Bold Condensed, Bookman Old Style, Times New Roman, New Times Roman PS, and Arabia.